SPOTLIGHT ON A FAIR AND EQUAL SOCIETY

JUSTICE FOR ALL

DANIELLE HAYNES

PowerKiDS press

Published in 2023 by The Rosen Publishing Group, Inc.
2544 Clinton Street, Buffalo, NY 14224

Copyright © 2023 by The Rosen Publishing Group, Inc.

All rights reserved. No part of this book may be reproduced in any form without permission in writing from the publisher, except by a reviewer.

First Edition

Editor: Greg Roza
Book Design: Michael Flynn
Interior Layout: Rachel Rising

Photo Credits: Cover Pixel-Shot/Shutterstock.com; Cover, pp. 1, 3–8, 10–14, 16–20, 22, 24–28, 30–32 tavizta/Shutterstock.com; pp. 4, 7, 17 Monkey Business Images/Shutterstock.com; p. 5 Library Company of Philadelphia; p. 9 Rena Schild/Shutterstock.com; p. 10 Roman Samborskyi/Shutterstock.com; p. 11 AnnaStills/Shutterstock.com; p. 12 Jacob Lund/Shutterstock.com; p. 13 Highsmith, Carol M., 1946-, photographer; p. 15 DisobeyArt/Shutterstocl.com; p. 16 ibreakstock/Shutterstock.com; p. 18 Dmitry Demidovich/Shutterstock.com; p. 19 Everett Collection/Shutterstock.com; p. 21 Jacob Lund/Shutterstock.com; p. 23 Nata Bene/Shutterstock.com; p. 24 fotogestoeber/Shutterstock.com; p. 25 Rawpixel.com/Shutterstock.com; p. 26 Lightspring/Shutterstock.com; p. 27 Halfpoint/Shutterstock.com; p. 29 https://commons.wikimedia.org/wiki/File:20190815_845a_Event_Technovation-Girls-2019_XE3_DSCF2730.jpg.

Library of Congress Cataloging-in-Publication Data

Names: Haynes, Danielle, author.
Title: Justice for all / Danielle Haynes.
Description: Buffalo, New York : PowerKids Press, [2023] | Series:
    Spotlight on a fair and equal society | Includes index.
Identifiers: LCCN 2022042703 (print) | LCCN 2022042704 (ebook) | ISBN
    9781538388235 (library binding) | ISBN 9781538388204 (paperback) | ISBN
    9781538388242 (ebook)
Subjects: LCSH: Social justice--Juvenile literature. | Equality--Juvenile
    literature.
Classification: LCC HM671 .H389 2023 (print) | LCC HM671 (ebook) | DDC
    340/.115--dc23/eng/20220923
LC record available at https://lccn.loc.gov/2022042703
LC ebook record available at https://lccn.loc.gov/2022042704

Manufactured in the United States of America

Some of the images in this book illustrate individuals who are models. The depictions do not imply actual situations or events.

CPSIA Compliance Information: Batch #CWPK23. For further information contact Rosen Publishing at 1-800-237-9932.

CONTENTS

SOCIAL JUSTICE CONNECTIONS. 4
WHAT IS FAIRNESS?. 6
WHERE DO YOU SEE INJUSTICE?. 8
YOUR SOCIAL IDENTITY. 10
SOCIAL JUSTICE AND RACE. 12
JUSTICE AT WORK. 14
SOCIAL JUSTICE AND MONEY 16
FAIRNESS IN ACTION 18
SOCIAL JUSTICE AND GENDER 20
THE IMPORTANCE OF EMPATHY 22
ADVANTAGES AND FAIRNESS. 24
TAKING ACTION NOW 26
GITANJALI RAO. 28
IMPROVING THE WORLD 30
GLOSSARY. 31
INDEX 32
PRIMARY SOURCE LIST .32

CHAPTER ONE
SOCIAL JUSTICE CONNECTIONS

To understand social justice in your real world, you can make connections with what you see and hear. In your class at school, justice means that every child has the safety they need. Does every child in your school or neighborhood have shoes, a winter coat, enough to eat, and health care? Justice means that every child has those things. In your town, does every child have a home? Does every child have the support they need to succeed in school? Does every child have the right to a bright future?

Educator and **activist** Emma Willard opened the first college for women in the United States—Troy Female Seminary—in 1821. After the success of her school, Willard spoke to people around the world about her teaching methods. Willard's efforts increased social justice for women all over the world.

    Social justice is happening close to home if you answer yes to these questions. Social injustice is happening close to home if you answer no. Seeing and hearing your real world with awareness and **empathy** builds a connection to your community.

CHAPTER TWO

WHAT IS FAIRNESS?

You probably know the difference between fair and unfair. Maybe you say, "That's not fair!" when a friend won't share. But what does fairness mean? Fairness means treating people equally. You understand what others need. You consider someone else's life with empathy.

There's a lot of unfairness—or injustice—in the world. Not everyone has the resources, opportunities, and basic rights they need to survive. This is unjust. Unfairness and injustice take many forms, including attitudes, speech, behavior, and laws. Social injustice happens when individuals or groups are treated differently because of their race, sexuality, age, **gender**, religion, or class. This is called discrimination.

Social justice happens when people work to end discrimination and unfairness. Social justice means that no one person has an unfair advantage or disadvantage compared to others.

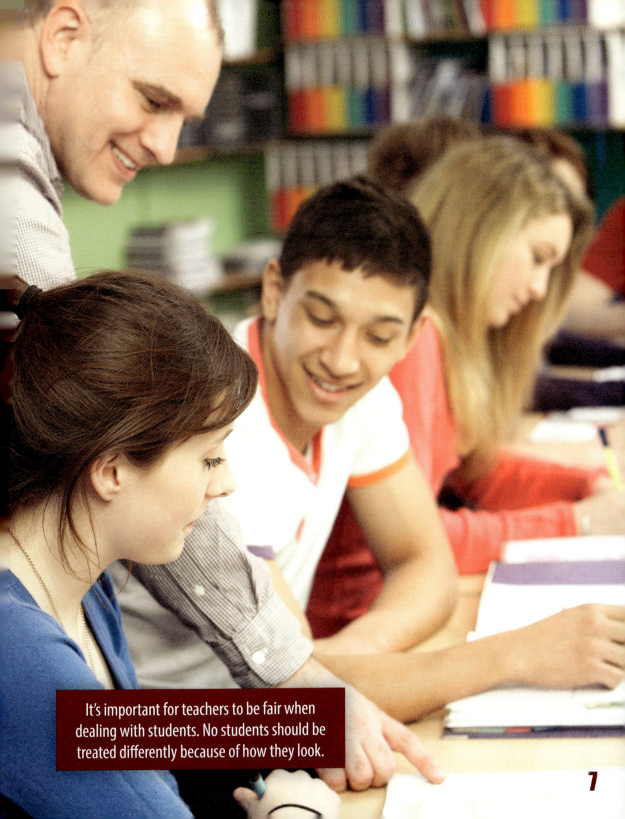

It's important for teachers to be fair when dealing with students. No students should be treated differently because of how they look.

7

CHAPTER THREE
WHERE DO YOU SEE INJUSTICE?

Social injustice is all around us in many forms. Sometimes it's easy to spot. Sometimes it's harder to see. Here are some examples:

- When children who are immigrants are bullied.
- When a woman is paid less to do the same job as a man.
- When Black people are treated unfairly if they are accused of breaking the law.
- When schools don't provide access for students in wheelchairs on the playground.
- When students who live in poverty can't afford to join sports or other activities.
- When laws keep some couples from getting married or adopting children.

These are all examples of social injustices that have really happened. Luckily, people have worked hard to fix them by passing laws. But some injustices still happen all the time and we must all stand up against them.

In the 2013 case *Obergefell v. Hodges*, the U.S. Supreme Court ruled that same-sex couples have the right to marry.

CHAPTER FOUR

YOUR SOCIAL IDENTITY

Social injustices often have connections to the most basic **characteristics** of a person. Some of these characteristics are visible, such as skin color and age, while others aren't so clear. The way people see you fitting into society impacts how people treat you—for better and worse.

Your social identity is the way you and other people think about how you fit into society. All of the identity groups that make you who you are combine to make up your social identity. Belonging to multiple identity groups is positive and shared by everyone. Often this is a source of pride, confidence, and healthy self-esteem.

There are lots of different factors that make up our social identity, including skin color, gender, sexual **orientation**, religion, age, and more.

Bias, discrimination, or **prejudice** can turn an aspect of your social identity into a negative. At the cost of respect, fairness, rights, and freedom, social injustice impacts your life.

CHAPTER FIVE
SOCIAL JUSTICE AND RACE

Social injustice affects many groups in our society. Black and brown people have experienced injustice in America for hundreds of years. They continue to experience it today even though many are working toward racial justice.

The history of racial injustice is long and painful. Starting with slavery, before America was even a nation, human beings lost all their rights and freedoms. To support the demand for labor, human beings were captured and enslaved in America.

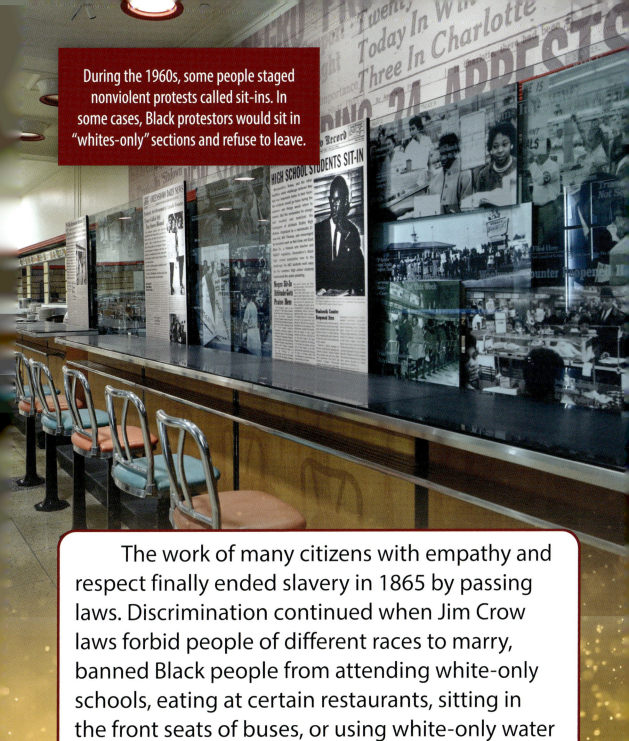

During the 1960s, some people staged nonviolent protests called sit-ins. In some cases, Black protestors would sit in "whites-only" sections and refuse to leave.

The work of many citizens with empathy and respect finally ended slavery in 1865 by passing laws. Discrimination continued when Jim Crow laws forbid people of different races to marry, banned Black people from attending white-only schools, eating at certain restaurants, sitting in the front seats of buses, or using white-only water fountains.

CHAPTER SIX

JUSTICE AT WORK

Many citizens believe in justice for all and work toward this goal. Allies organize their efforts, speak up, and take action against injustice. They raise awareness of injustice, protest against it, and change bad laws. This is true today and it is also true of our past.

Social justice movements have been a force in ending **segregation**, protecting voting rights, and fighting for criminal justice. The civil rights movement in the 1950s and 1960s had leaders like Martin Luther King Jr. and thousands of supporters throughout the country who took part in marches, **boycotts**, and sit-ins.

A series of killings of unarmed Black Americans in the 2010s led to protests and more calls for social justice. This social justice movement condemns unjust killings and calls for society to value the lives of Black people.

Widespread anti-racism protests have taken place across the globe over the past decade.

CHAPTER SEVEN
SOCIAL JUSTICE AND MONEY

The fact that many Americans live in poverty leads to injustice. The basic needs of food, clothing, shelter, and transportation cost more money than one out of six Americans has. Poverty can cause unfair disadvantages such as living where there is poor air quality or lower quality schools. Poverty is often a cause of **barriers** to health care, nutritious food, or opportunities that many others have. This is economic injustice.

It's not always easy to know a person's **socioeconomic** status just by looking at them, so it's a good idea to remember that your classmates may have different home lives than you.

You can't control where you live or your family income. If your parents have good jobs, you'll likely live in a bigger home and nicer neighborhood. You'll probably go to a quality school. It's more likely you'll have the support you need for a better education and start a career. These advantages can be used to end poverty, share your resources, and take action.

17

CHAPTER EIGHT

FAIRNESS IN ACTION

Leaders, volunteers, and citizens have worked for economic justice. Social justice means everyone—no matter where they live or how much money they make—should have equal access to good education, health care, legal help, and jobs.

In the 1930s, America was in a terrible economic crisis—12,830,000 Americans were out of work. President Franklin D. Roosevelt's New Deal helped put millions of people to work building roads, fighting forest fires, and planting trees. The program helped the people most affected by the Great **Depression**.

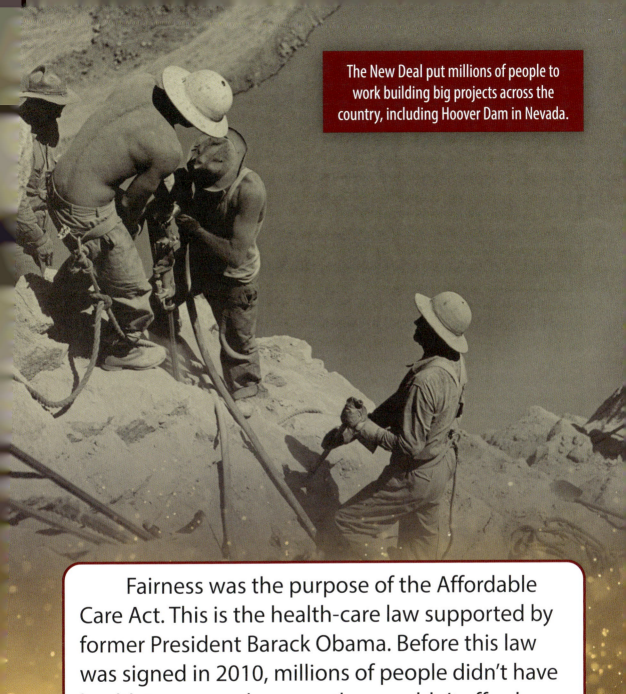

The New Deal put millions of people to work building big projects across the country, including Hoover Dam in Nevada.

Fairness was the purpose of the Affordable Care Act. This is the health-care law supported by former President Barack Obama. Before this law was signed in 2010, millions of people didn't have health insurance because they couldn't afford it. Without insurance, they couldn't see a doctor when they were sick.

CHAPTER NINE

SOCIAL JUSTICE AND GENDER

Biased words, behaviors, and laws limit rights and freedoms of people based on gender. Women experienced injustice for centuries. Their rights to work, own property, go to school, vote, and marry as they chose were all out of reach. Today girls and women still struggle with these injustices although laws have caused changes.

Gender bias affects men who want to stay home with a newborn child. Companies began to give dads leave to be a new parent. Some dads stay home and take care of families while their wives work and support them. This supports rights and freedom.

Some laws affect the rights of those who choose to marry people who are the same gender as themselves. People with different gender identities face barriers and bias in their lives. Many are working to change this injustice.

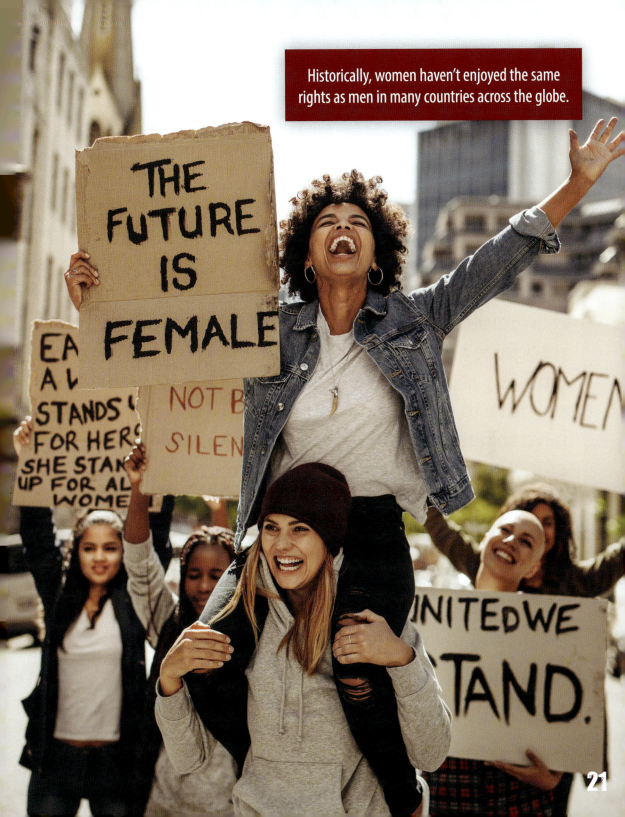

Historically, women haven't enjoyed the same rights as men in many countries across the globe.

CHAPTER TEN
THE IMPORTANCE OF EMPATHY

A society with social justice is a fair society. Perhaps you want to stop injustices in your life and the lives of others. But how do you start? The first step is to learn how to recognize injustice.

Empathy is a great tool for helping you recognize and take action against social injustice. Empathy is the ability to understand or be sensitive to another person's feelings. You don't have to have the same experiences to have empathy for another person. The more you surround yourself with people who have different social identities, the more you'll learn about their different experiences. That knowledge will make it easier for you to pick up on social injustices. It may also inspire you to act to make the world a better place for you, your friends, and even strangers.

Having empathy for those around you will help you understand their thoughts and feelings.

23

CHAPTER ELEVEN
ADVANTAGES AND FAIRNESS

Two girls from nice homes are chatting about the mansions they plan to live in when they grow up. They may not be aware of their advantages or the disadvantages of others.

Growing into awareness of fairness and unfairness in society takes experience and relationships outside your own identity group. Listening to others and feeling empathy for them is the doorway to understanding social justice. You can begin to see who has enough, who has more than they need, and who does not have enough.

People who have advantages have a responsibility to use them to help bring about social justice.

    Once you start noticing unfairness, discrimination, and disadvantages, you can begin to see yourself as someone who can be an agent of change. You can begin to use your advantages or those of your peers to make your real world a fair place.

CHAPTER TWELVE

TAKING ACTION NOW

When you recognize injustice, the first thing you can do is use your voice. You can respectfully tell someone when their words or actions are biased or hurtful. When you see unfairness, you can speak up or take action.

Have you seen an injustice at school? What if some students did not have the technology they needed for school work? Maybe they need to borrow Chromebooks or take home a Wi-Fi hotspot. Decide on a goal. You can work with others to plan and coordinate actions. Allies are key to success.

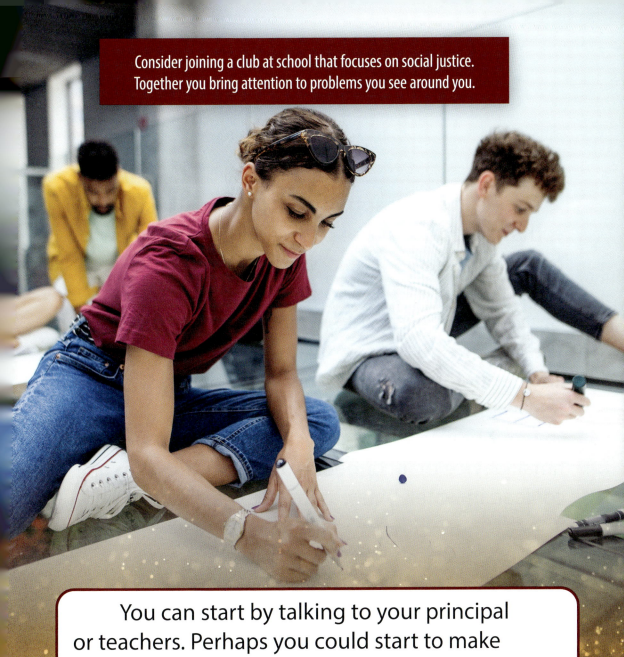

Consider joining a club at school that focuses on social justice. Together you bring attention to problems you see around you.

You can start by talking to your principal or teachers. Perhaps you could start to make the community aware of the problem. Signs, posters, flyers, or letters could reach many people. Perhaps you can convince local organizations to donate laptops.

27

CHAPTER THIRTEEN

GITANJALI RAO

One of the best things about social justice is that anyone can take part, regardless of your background, age, race, or ability. Take Gitanjali Rao, for instance.

At just 15 years old, *Time* magazine named Gitanjali the "Kid of the Year" for 2020. She earned the honor for creating technology to help solve social injustices. One of her most important inventions was something called Tethys. It's a small device that connects to a smartphone to test for lead in water. She was just 11 years old when she came up with the idea!

Gitanjali said she was inspired to create the device when she learned about the Flint, Michigan, water **crisis**. In 2014, people in the city began getting lead poisoning from the water. The crisis mostly affected people of color in poorer neighborhoods.

Gitanjali Rao was just 11 years old when she invented a device and app to test for lead in water.

CHAPTER FOURTEEN

IMPROVING THE WORLD

Taking action to bring about social justice is an important part of being a member of any community. We should all take part in the process to end inequality and discrimination. Think about times when you've been treated unfairly. It probably didn't feel very good. Hopefully, it doesn't feel very good when you think about others being treated unfairly, too.

Keep in mind that social injustices can happen in your everyday life at school. Do you notice some students are treated unfairly with words, attitudes, or actions? Speak up and bring it to the attention of a trusted adult. Changing injustice even on a small level brings about fairness for everyone.

But social injustice also happens on a wider scale, even at the government level. What can you do to make a difference for yourself and everyone around you?

GLOSSARY

activist (AK-tuh-vist) Someone who acts strongly in support of or against an issue.

barrier (BAA-ree-uhr) Something that stops something else from happening or passing.

bias (BY-uhs) Prejudice either against or in favor of another person, usually unfairly.

boycott (BOY-kaht) A refusal to buy, use, or participate in something.

characteristic (kayr-ack-tuh-RIH-stik) A special quality that makes a person, thing, or group different from others.

crisis (KRY-sihs) A difficult or dangerous situation that needs serious attention.

depression (dih-PREH-shun) A period of low economic activity marked by rising levels of unemployment.

empathy (EHM-puh-thee) The understanding and sharing of the emotions and experiences of another person.

gender (JEN-duhr) The set of social expectations or traits men or women are expected to meet or have.

orientation (or-ee-ihn-TAY-shuhn) A person's sexual identity.

prejudice (PREH-juh-diss) An unfair feeling of dislike for a person or group because of race or religious or political beliefs.

segregation (seh-grih-GAY-shuhn) The separation of people based on race, class, or ethnicity.

socioeconomic (SOH-see-oh-eh-koh-NAH-mihk) Relating to a combination of social and economic factors.

INDEX

A
Affordable Care Act, 19
age, 6, 10, 11

B
bias, 11, 20, 26
boycott, 14

D
disability, 8
discrimination, 13, 25, 30
Durham, North Carolina, 13

E
education, 5, 7, 13, 18, 20, 26, 27
empathy, 5, 6, 13, 22, 23, 24

G
gender, 5, 6, 8, 11, 20, 21
Great Depression, 18

H
health care, 4, 16, 18, 19
Hoover Dam, 19

I
immigrants, 8

J
Jim Crow, 13

K
King, Martin Luther, Jr., 14

L
laws, 8, 13, 14, 20
lead poisoning, 28, 29

N
New Deal, 18, 19

O
Obama, Barack, 19
Obergefell v. Hodges, 9

P
poverty, 8, 16, 17, 18, 19, 24, 26, 28
protest, 13, 14, 15

R
race, 6, 8, 10, 11, 12, 13, 14, 15, 28
Rao, Gitanjali, 28, 29
religion, 6, 11
Roosevelt, Franklin D., 18, 19

S
segregation, 13, 14
sexuality, 6, 8, 9, 11
sit-in, 13, 13
slavery, 12, 13
smartphone, 28, 29
social identity, 10, 11, 22, 24
Supreme Court (U.S.), 9

V
voting rights, 14, 20

PRIMARY SOURCE LIST

Page 5
Willard, Emma, 1787-1870. Wood engraving. John William Orr. Circa 1855. Library Company of Philadelphia.

Page 13
Lunch counter at the old Woolworth's "five and dime" store, now part of the International Civil Rights Center & Museum. Photo. June 12, 2017. Carol M. Highsmith. Held by Library of Congress.

Page 19
Four workers build the Hoover Dam above the Colorado River. Photograph. 1934. Nevada. Held by the Everett Collection.